# I Am a Little Pastry Chef

Mayumi Oono

# We need some tools to bake:

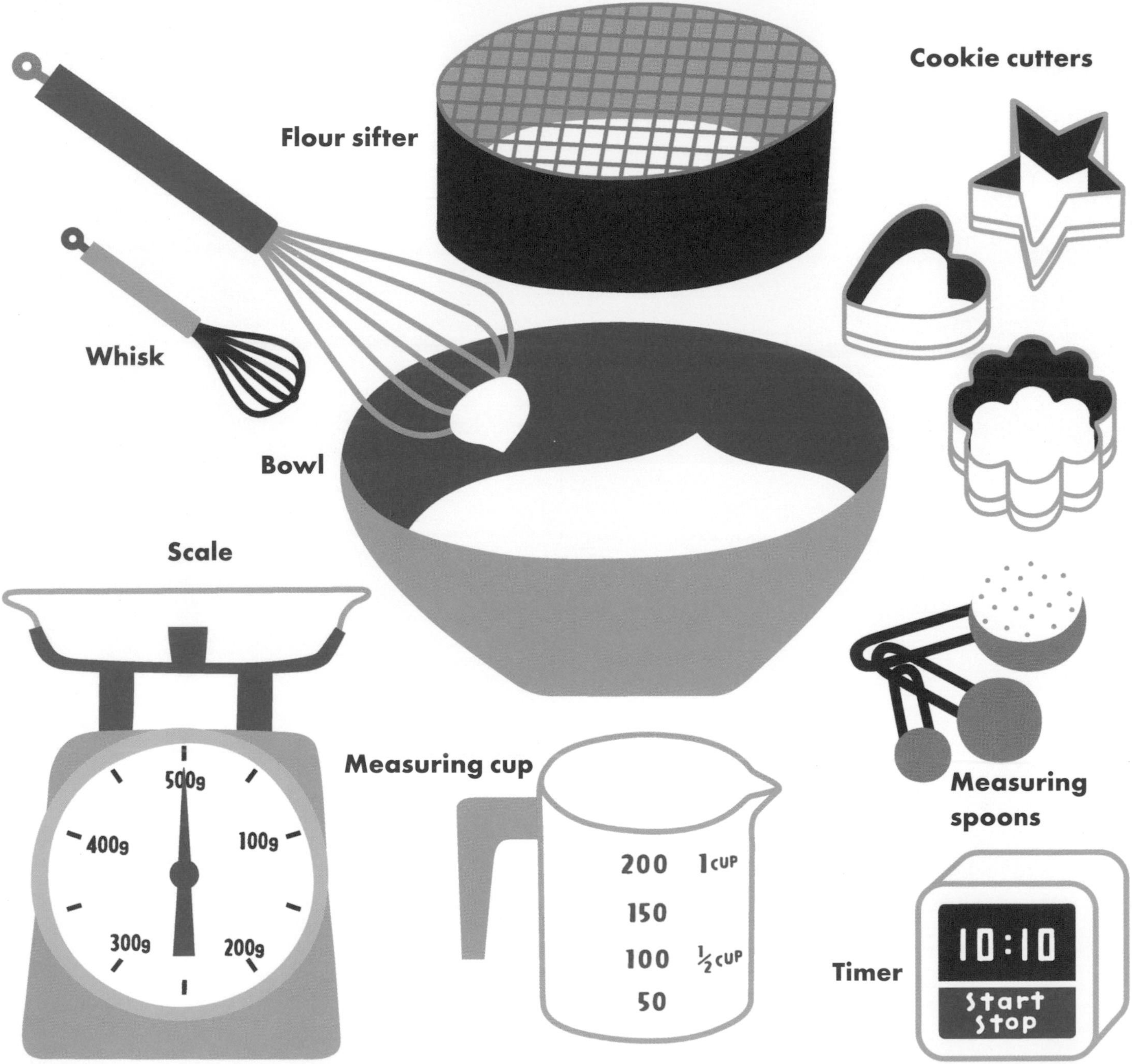

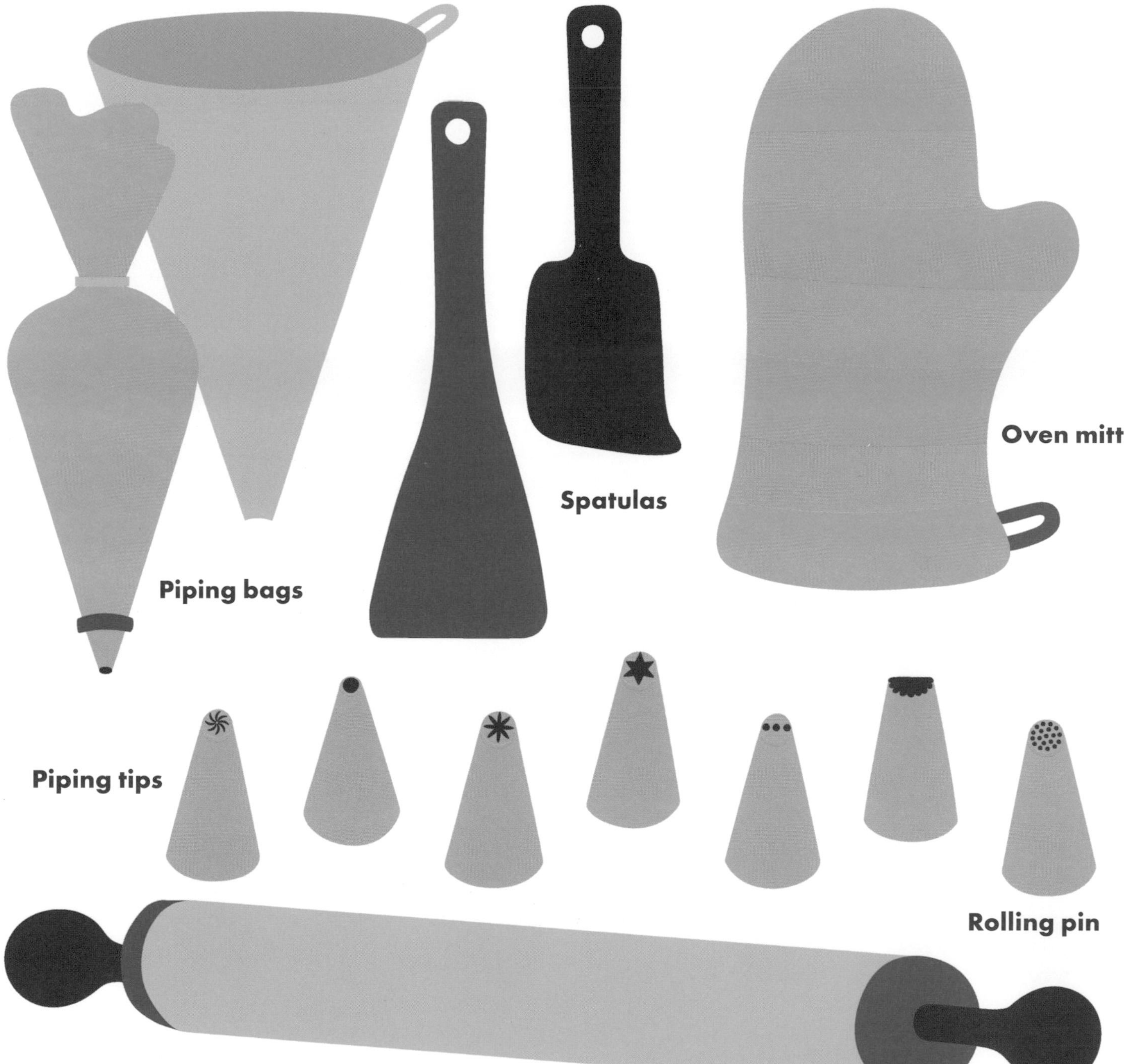
Piping bags
Spatulas
Oven mitt
Piping tips
Rolling pin

What should we bake today? First, choose a dessert...

Chocolate
lava cake
Cupcakes
Macarons
Cookies

## Then, choose a flavor.

Raspberry

Mint

Orange

Vanilla

Maple

Strawberry

Coffee

Apricot

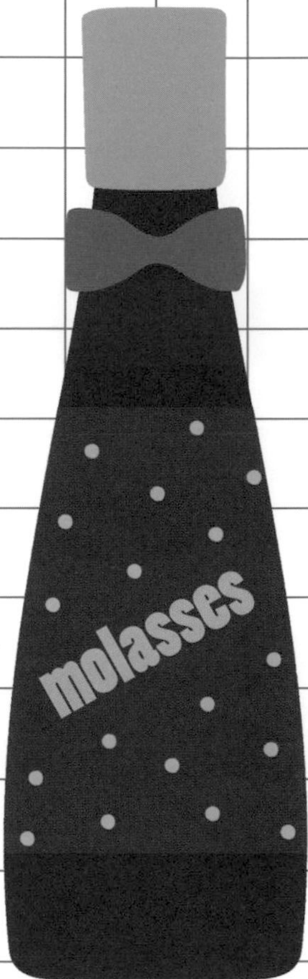


Molasses

Green tea

Chocolate

Black currant

To bake a cake, you need to mix the ingredients.

**This is the fun part—cutting the dough with cookie cutters!**

**If you want to bake muffins,**
**it's time to fill the muffin tins.**

**Now let's bake them!**

## Complete your creations with delicious decorations!

**Decorate the frosting on these cupcakes.**

**Add some frosting...**

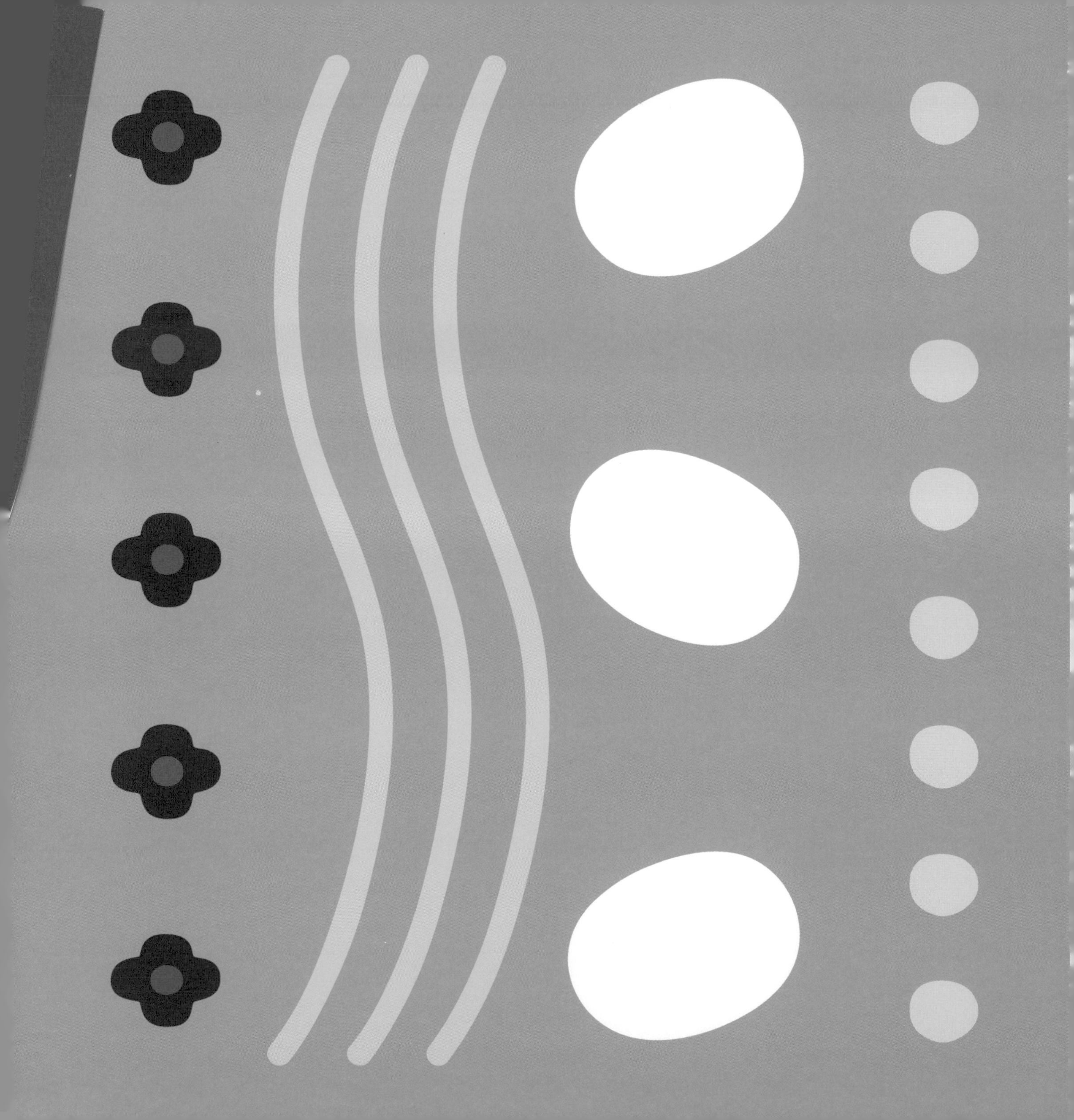

Decorate these cookies with frosting!

Decorate these desserts!

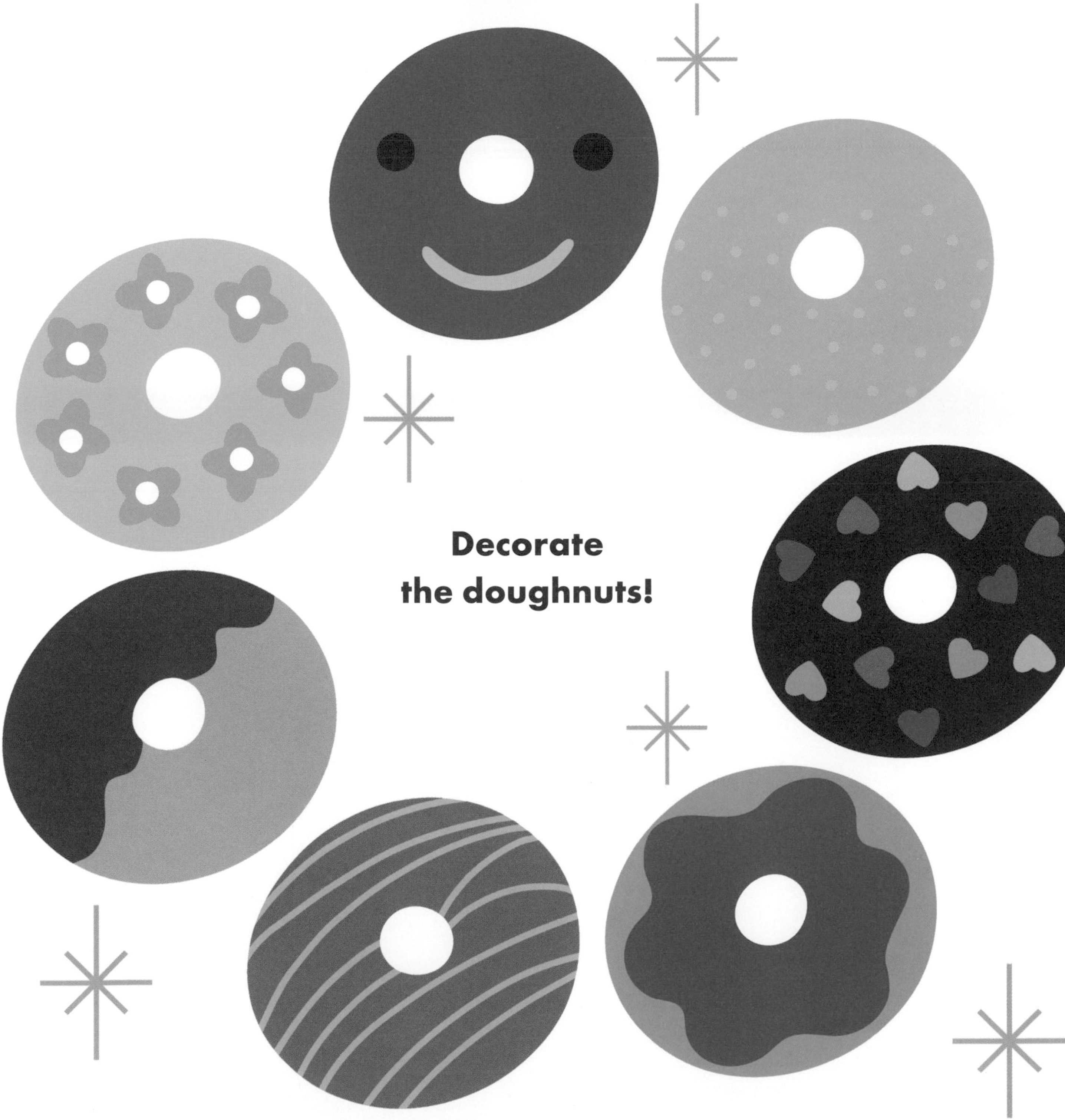
Decorate
the doughnuts!

# Decorate the cakes!

*Special thanks to Mika Ogawa (Micarina).—MO*

*Little Professionals: I Am a Little Pastry Chef* first published
in the United States by Tra Publishing 2022


Original title: *La meva petita pastisseria*

Printed and bound in China
ISBN: 978-1-7347618-4-9

*Little Professionals: I Am a Little Pastry Chef* is printed on Forest Stewardship
Council certified paper from well-managed forests.
Tra Publishing is committed to sustainability in its materials and practices.

FSC www.fsc.org MIX Paper from responsible sources FSC® C102842

Tra Publishing
245 NE 37th Street
Miami, FL 33137
trapublishing.com

tra.publishing